50 Casseroles for Every Occasion
Recipes for Home

By: Kelly Johnson

Table of Contents

- Classic Tuna Noodle Casserole
- Chicken and Rice Casserole
- Beef Stroganoff Casserole
- Baked Ziti with Italian Sausage
- Broccoli Cheese Casserole
- Enchilada Casserole
- Shepherd's Pie
- Macaroni and Cheese Casserole
- Vegetable Lasagna
- Ham and Potato Casserole
- Quinoa and Black Bean Casserole
- Sweet Potato and Chicken Casserole
- Eggplant Parmesan Casserole
- Stuffed Pepper Casserole
- Chili Mac Casserole
- Cornbread and Sausage Casserole
- Mediterranean Chickpea Casserole
- Pesto Chicken and Rice Casserole
- Buffalo Chicken Casserole
- Mexican Street Corn Casserole
- Seafood Pasta Bake
- Breakfast Casserole with Sausage
- Spinach and Feta Casserole
- Baked Creamed Spinach Casserole
- Italian Meatball Casserole
- Cranberry Chicken Casserole
- Loaded Baked Potato Casserole
- Ratatouille Casserole
- BBQ Chicken Casserole
- Sloppy Joe Casserole
- Pizza Pasta Casserole
- Chicken Pot Pie Casserole
- Cabbage Roll Casserole
- Wild Rice and Mushroom Casserole
- Shrimp and Grits Casserole

- Zucchini and Tomato Casserole
- French Onion Soup Casserole
- Apple and Sausage Stuffing Casserole
- Lentil and Vegetable Casserole
- Chocolate Chip Cookie Dough Casserole
- Cranberry and Orange Breakfast Casserole
- Butternut Squash and Kale Casserole
- Greek Pastitsio Casserole
- Coconut Curry Rice Casserole
- Beef and Bean Enchilada Casserole
- Caprese Pasta Casserole
- Poppy Seed Chicken Casserole
- Thai Peanut Chicken Casserole
- Pumpkin and Sage Casserole
- Teriyaki Chicken Casserole

Classic Tuna Noodle Casserole

Ingredients:

- 8 oz egg noodles
- 2 cans (5 oz each) tuna, drained
- 1 can (10.5 oz) cream of mushroom soup
- 1 cup frozen peas
- 1 cup milk
- 1 cup shredded cheddar cheese
- 1/2 cup breadcrumbs
- Salt and pepper (to taste)
- 1 tablespoon olive oil

Instructions:

1. **Preheat Oven**: Preheat the oven to 350°F (175°C).
2. **Cook Noodles**: Boil the egg noodles according to package instructions. Drain and set aside.
3. **Mix Ingredients**: In a large bowl, combine cooked noodles, tuna, cream of mushroom soup, peas, milk, half of the cheddar cheese, salt, and pepper.
4. **Transfer to Dish**: Pour the mixture into a greased 9x13-inch baking dish.
5. **Top with Cheese and Breadcrumbs**: Sprinkle the remaining cheese and breadcrumbs on top, then drizzle with olive oil.
6. **Bake**: Bake for 25-30 minutes, or until bubbly and golden brown.

Chicken and Rice Casserole

Ingredients:

- 2 cups cooked rice
- 2 cups cooked chicken, shredded
- 1 can (10.5 oz) cream of chicken soup
- 1 cup chicken broth
- 1 cup frozen mixed vegetables
- 1 cup shredded cheddar cheese
- Salt and pepper (to taste)
- 1/2 teaspoon garlic powder

Instructions:

1. **Preheat Oven**: Preheat the oven to 350°F (175°C).
2. **Combine Ingredients**: In a large bowl, mix cooked rice, chicken, cream of chicken soup, chicken broth, mixed vegetables, garlic powder, salt, and pepper.
3. **Transfer to Dish**: Pour the mixture into a greased 9x13-inch baking dish.
4. **Top with Cheese**: Sprinkle cheese on top.
5. **Bake**: Bake for 30-35 minutes, or until heated through and bubbly.

Beef Stroganoff Casserole

Ingredients:

- 1 lb ground beef
- 1 onion, chopped
- 2 cups egg noodles
- 1 can (10.5 oz) cream of mushroom soup
- 1 cup beef broth
- 1 tablespoon Worcestershire sauce
- 1 cup sour cream
- Salt and pepper (to taste)
- 1 cup shredded cheddar cheese

Instructions:

1. **Preheat Oven**: Preheat the oven to 350°F (175°C).
2. **Cook Noodles**: Boil the egg noodles according to package instructions. Drain and set aside.
3. **Brown Beef**: In a skillet, brown the ground beef and onion until fully cooked. Drain excess fat.
4. **Combine Ingredients**: In a large bowl, mix cooked noodles, beef mixture, cream of mushroom soup, beef broth, Worcestershire sauce, salt, and pepper.
5. **Transfer to Dish**: Pour the mixture into a greased 9x13-inch baking dish.
6. **Top with Sour Cream and Cheese**: Spread sour cream on top and sprinkle with cheese.
7. **Bake**: Bake for 25-30 minutes until hot and bubbly.

Baked Ziti with Italian Sausage

Ingredients:

- 12 oz ziti pasta
- 1 lb Italian sausage, casing removed
- 1 jar (24 oz) marinara sauce
- 2 cups ricotta cheese
- 2 cups shredded mozzarella cheese
- 1/2 cup grated Parmesan cheese
- 1 teaspoon Italian seasoning
- Salt and pepper (to taste)

Instructions:

1. **Preheat Oven**: Preheat the oven to 375°F (190°C).
2. **Cook Pasta**: Boil ziti according to package instructions. Drain and set aside.
3. **Cook Sausage**: In a skillet, cook Italian sausage until browned. Drain excess fat.
4. **Combine Ingredients**: In a large bowl, mix cooked ziti, sausage, marinara sauce, ricotta cheese, Italian seasoning, salt, and pepper.
5. **Transfer to Dish**: Pour the mixture into a greased 9x13-inch baking dish.
6. **Top with Cheese**: Sprinkle mozzarella and Parmesan cheese on top.
7. **Bake**: Bake for 25-30 minutes until cheese is melted and bubbly.

Broccoli Cheese Casserole

Ingredients:

- 4 cups broccoli florets (fresh or frozen)
- 1 can (10.5 oz) cream of mushroom soup
- 1 cup mayonnaise
- 1 cup shredded cheddar cheese
- 1/2 cup breadcrumbs
- Salt and pepper (to taste)

Instructions:

1. **Preheat Oven**: Preheat the oven to 350°F (175°C).
2. **Blanch Broccoli**: If using fresh broccoli, blanch in boiling water for 2-3 minutes, then drain.
3. **Combine Ingredients**: In a large bowl, mix broccoli, cream of mushroom soup, mayonnaise, half of the cheddar cheese, salt, and pepper.
4. **Transfer to Dish**: Pour the mixture into a greased 9x13-inch baking dish.
5. **Top with Cheese and Breadcrumbs**: Sprinkle remaining cheese and breadcrumbs on top.
6. **Bake**: Bake for 25-30 minutes until hot and bubbly.

Enchilada Casserole

Ingredients:

- 12 corn tortillas
- 2 cups shredded chicken or beef
- 1 can (10 oz) enchilada sauce
- 2 cups shredded cheese (Mexican blend or cheddar)
- 1 can (15 oz) black beans, drained and rinsed
- 1 cup corn (canned or frozen)
- Optional toppings: sour cream, avocado, cilantro

Instructions:

1. **Preheat Oven**: Preheat the oven to 350°F (175°C).
2. **Layer Ingredients**: In a greased 9x13-inch baking dish, layer 4 tortillas, half of the meat, half of the enchilada sauce, half of the beans, half of the corn, and a third of the cheese. Repeat the layers.
3. **Top with Remaining Cheese**: Finish with a layer of tortillas and the remaining cheese on top.
4. **Bake**: Bake for 25-30 minutes until cheese is bubbly and golden.
5. **Serve**: Top with optional garnishes before serving.

Shepherd's Pie

Ingredients:

- 1 lb ground lamb or beef
- 1 onion, chopped
- 2 cups mixed vegetables (carrots, peas, corn)
- 1 cup beef broth
- 2 cups mashed potatoes (store-bought or homemade)
- 1 teaspoon Worcestershire sauce
- Salt and pepper (to taste)
- Olive oil

Instructions:

1. **Preheat Oven**: Preheat the oven to 400°F (200°C).
2. **Brown Meat**: In a skillet, heat olive oil over medium heat. Add ground meat and onion, cooking until browned. Drain excess fat.
3. **Add Vegetables**: Stir in mixed vegetables, beef broth, Worcestershire sauce, salt, and pepper. Simmer for about 5 minutes.
4. **Transfer to Dish**: Pour the meat mixture into a greased 9x13-inch baking dish.
5. **Top with Mashed Potatoes**: Spread mashed potatoes over the meat mixture evenly.
6. **Bake**: Bake for 25-30 minutes until the top is golden and bubbling.

Macaroni and Cheese Casserole

Ingredients:

- 8 oz elbow macaroni
- 2 cups shredded cheese (cheddar, Monterey Jack, or a blend)
- 2 cups milk
- 1/4 cup butter
- 1/4 cup all-purpose flour
- 1 teaspoon mustard powder (optional)
- Salt and pepper (to taste)
- 1/2 cup breadcrumbs (optional)

Instructions:

1. **Preheat Oven**: Preheat the oven to 350°F (175°C).
2. **Cook Macaroni**: Boil macaroni according to package instructions. Drain and set aside.
3. **Make Cheese Sauce**: In a saucepan, melt butter over medium heat. Stir in flour and cook for 1 minute. Gradually whisk in milk and cook until thickened. Stir in cheese, mustard powder, salt, and pepper until melted.
4. **Combine Ingredients**: In a large bowl, mix cooked macaroni with cheese sauce.
5. **Transfer to Dish**: Pour into a greased 9x13-inch baking dish and sprinkle breadcrumbs on top if using.
6. **Bake**: Bake for 25-30 minutes until golden and bubbly.

These comforting casseroles are perfect for family meals or gatherings! Enjoy!

Vegetable Lasagna

Ingredients:

- 9 lasagna noodles
- 2 cups ricotta cheese
- 2 cups marinara sauce
- 2 cups mixed vegetables (zucchini, spinach, mushrooms)
- 2 cups shredded mozzarella cheese
- 1/2 cup grated Parmesan cheese
- 1 egg
- Salt and pepper (to taste)
- 1 teaspoon Italian seasoning

Instructions:

1. **Preheat Oven**: Preheat the oven to 375°F (190°C).
2. **Cook Noodles**: Boil lasagna noodles according to package instructions. Drain and set aside.
3. **Mix Cheese Filling**: In a bowl, combine ricotta cheese, egg, Italian seasoning, salt, and pepper.
4. **Layer Ingredients**: In a greased 9x13-inch baking dish, spread a layer of marinara sauce, followed by 3 noodles, half of the ricotta mixture, half of the mixed vegetables, and a third of the mozzarella. Repeat layers, ending with noodles and marinara on top. Sprinkle remaining mozzarella and Parmesan.
5. **Bake**: Cover with foil and bake for 30 minutes. Remove foil and bake for an additional 15-20 minutes until bubbly and golden.
6. **Cool and Serve**: Let cool for a few minutes before slicing and serving.

Ham and Potato Casserole

Ingredients:

- 4 cups diced potatoes (fresh or frozen)
- 2 cups diced ham
- 1 can (10.5 oz) cream of chicken soup
- 1 cup milk
- 1 cup shredded cheddar cheese
- 1/2 cup chopped onion
- Salt and pepper (to taste)

Instructions:

1. **Preheat Oven**: Preheat the oven to 350°F (175°C).
2. **Combine Ingredients**: In a large bowl, mix diced potatoes, ham, cream of chicken soup, milk, onion, salt, and pepper.
3. **Transfer to Dish**: Pour the mixture into a greased 9x13-inch baking dish and spread evenly.
4. **Top with Cheese**: Sprinkle cheese on top.
5. **Bake**: Cover with foil and bake for 45 minutes. Remove foil and bake for an additional 15 minutes until potatoes are tender and cheese is bubbly.

Quinoa and Black Bean Casserole

Ingredients:

- 1 cup quinoa, rinsed
- 2 cups vegetable broth
- 1 can (15 oz) black beans, drained and rinsed
- 1 cup corn (canned or frozen)
- 1 jar (16 oz) salsa
- 1 teaspoon cumin
- 1 cup shredded cheese (cheddar or Monterey Jack)
- Salt and pepper (to taste)

Instructions:

1. **Preheat Oven**: Preheat the oven to 350°F (175°C).
2. **Cook Quinoa**: In a saucepan, bring vegetable broth to a boil. Add quinoa, cover, and simmer for 15 minutes until liquid is absorbed.
3. **Combine Ingredients**: In a large bowl, mix cooked quinoa, black beans, corn, salsa, cumin, salt, and pepper.
4. **Transfer to Dish**: Pour into a greased 9x13-inch baking dish and spread evenly.
5. **Top with Cheese**: Sprinkle cheese on top.
6. **Bake**: Bake for 25-30 minutes until heated through and cheese is melted.

Sweet Potato and Chicken Casserole

Ingredients:

- 2 cups cooked chicken, shredded
- 2 cups sweet potatoes, diced (fresh or frozen)
- 1 can (10.5 oz) cream of chicken soup
- 1 cup chicken broth
- 1 cup shredded cheddar cheese
- 1 teaspoon thyme
- Salt and pepper (to taste)

Instructions:

1. **Preheat Oven**: Preheat the oven to 350°F (175°C).
2. **Combine Ingredients**: In a large bowl, mix shredded chicken, sweet potatoes, cream of chicken soup, chicken broth, thyme, salt, and pepper.
3. **Transfer to Dish**: Pour into a greased 9x13-inch baking dish and spread evenly.
4. **Top with Cheese**: Sprinkle cheese on top.
5. **Bake**: Bake for 40-45 minutes until sweet potatoes are tender and cheese is bubbly.

Eggplant Parmesan Casserole

Ingredients:

- 2 medium eggplants, sliced
- 3 cups marinara sauce
- 2 cups shredded mozzarella cheese
- 1 cup grated Parmesan cheese
- 1 cup breadcrumbs
- Olive oil
- Salt and pepper (to taste)

Instructions:

1. **Preheat Oven**: Preheat the oven to 375°F (190°C).
2. **Prepare Eggplant**: Sprinkle eggplant slices with salt and let sit for 30 minutes to draw out moisture. Rinse and pat dry.
3. **Layer Ingredients**: In a greased 9x13-inch baking dish, layer eggplant, marinara sauce, mozzarella, and Parmesan. Repeat layers, finishing with marinara and a topping of breadcrumbs.
4. **Drizzle with Olive Oil**: Lightly drizzle olive oil over the breadcrumbs.
5. **Bake**: Bake for 35-40 minutes until golden and bubbly.

Stuffed Pepper Casserole

Ingredients:

- 4 bell peppers, chopped
- 1 lb ground beef or turkey
- 1 cup cooked rice
- 1 can (15 oz) diced tomatoes
- 1 cup shredded cheese (cheddar or mozzarella)
- 1 teaspoon Italian seasoning
- Salt and pepper (to taste)

Instructions:

1. **Preheat Oven**: Preheat the oven to 350°F (175°C).
2. **Cook Meat**: In a skillet, brown ground meat with bell peppers until cooked through. Drain excess fat.
3. **Combine Ingredients**: In a large bowl, mix cooked meat and peppers with cooked rice, diced tomatoes, Italian seasoning, salt, and pepper.
4. **Transfer to Dish**: Pour into a greased 9x13-inch baking dish.
5. **Top with Cheese**: Sprinkle cheese on top.
6. **Bake**: Bake for 25-30 minutes until heated through and cheese is melted.

Chili Mac Casserole

Ingredients:

- 1 lb ground beef
- 1 can (15 oz) chili (with or without beans)
- 2 cups elbow macaroni
- 2 cups shredded cheese (cheddar or a blend)
- 1 can (14.5 oz) diced tomatoes
- 1 cup beef broth
- Salt and pepper (to taste)

Instructions:

1. **Preheat Oven**: Preheat the oven to 350°F (175°C).
2. **Cook Macaroni**: Boil macaroni according to package instructions. Drain and set aside.
3. **Brown Beef**: In a skillet, brown ground beef. Drain excess fat.
4. **Combine Ingredients**: In a large bowl, mix cooked macaroni, beef, chili, diced tomatoes, beef broth, salt, and pepper.
5. **Transfer to Dish**: Pour into a greased 9x13-inch baking dish.
6. **Top with Cheese**: Sprinkle cheese on top.
7. **Bake**: Bake for 25-30 minutes until bubbly and golden.

Cornbread and Sausage Casserole

Ingredients:

- 1 lb breakfast sausage
- 1 box (8.5 oz) cornbread mix
- 1 cup milk
- 2 eggs
- 1 cup shredded cheese (cheddar or your choice)
- 1/2 cup chopped onion
- Salt and pepper (to taste)

Instructions:

1. **Preheat Oven**: Preheat the oven to 350°F (175°C).
2. **Cook Sausage**: In a skillet, brown sausage with onion until fully cooked. Drain excess fat.
3. **Prepare Cornbread Mixture**: In a bowl, combine cornbread mix, milk, eggs, salt, and pepper.
4. **Combine Ingredients**: Stir in cooked sausage and half of the cheese.
5. **Transfer to Dish**: Pour into a greased 9x13-inch baking dish.
6. **Top with Remaining Cheese**: Sprinkle remaining cheese on top.
7. **Bake**: Bake for 25-30 minutes until golden and a toothpick comes out clean.

These delicious casseroles are perfect for any meal! Enjoy!

Mediterranean Chickpea Casserole

Ingredients:

- 2 cans (15 oz each) chickpeas, drained and rinsed
- 1 can (14.5 oz) diced tomatoes
- 1 cup cooked quinoa or rice
- 1 cup chopped spinach
- 1/2 cup Kalamata olives, pitted and sliced
- 1/2 cup crumbled feta cheese
- 1 teaspoon dried oregano
- 1 teaspoon garlic powder
- Salt and pepper (to taste)
- Olive oil

Instructions:

1. **Preheat Oven**: Preheat the oven to 375°F (190°C).
2. **Combine Ingredients**: In a large bowl, mix chickpeas, diced tomatoes, cooked quinoa or rice, spinach, olives, feta, oregano, garlic powder, salt, and pepper.
3. **Transfer to Dish**: Pour the mixture into a greased 9x13-inch baking dish.
4. **Drizzle with Olive Oil**: Lightly drizzle olive oil over the top.
5. **Bake**: Bake for 25-30 minutes until heated through.

Pesto Chicken and Rice Casserole

Ingredients:

- 2 cups cooked chicken, shredded
- 1 cup cooked rice
- 1 cup pesto sauce
- 1 cup shredded mozzarella cheese
- 1/2 cup cherry tomatoes, halved
- Salt and pepper (to taste)

Instructions:

1. **Preheat Oven**: Preheat the oven to 350°F (175°C).
2. **Combine Ingredients**: In a large bowl, mix shredded chicken, cooked rice, pesto, half of the mozzarella, cherry tomatoes, salt, and pepper.
3. **Transfer to Dish**: Pour the mixture into a greased 9x13-inch baking dish.
4. **Top with Cheese**: Sprinkle the remaining mozzarella on top.
5. **Bake**: Bake for 25-30 minutes until heated through and cheese is bubbly.

Buffalo Chicken Casserole

Ingredients:

- 2 cups cooked chicken, shredded
- 1 cup buffalo sauce
- 1 cup cooked pasta (corkscrew or penne)
- 1 cup ranch dressing
- 1 cup shredded cheddar cheese
- 1/2 cup chopped green onions

Instructions:

1. **Preheat Oven**: Preheat the oven to 350°F (175°C).
2. **Combine Ingredients**: In a large bowl, mix shredded chicken, buffalo sauce, cooked pasta, ranch dressing, half of the cheddar cheese, and green onions.
3. **Transfer to Dish**: Pour into a greased 9x13-inch baking dish.
4. **Top with Cheese**: Sprinkle remaining cheese on top.
5. **Bake**: Bake for 25-30 minutes until heated through and cheese is melted.

Mexican Street Corn Casserole

Ingredients:

- 4 cups corn (fresh, frozen, or canned)
- 1/2 cup mayonnaise
- 1/2 cup sour cream
- 1 cup crumbled cotija cheese
- 1 tablespoon lime juice
- 1 teaspoon chili powder
- 1/2 teaspoon garlic powder
- Salt and pepper (to taste)
- 1/4 cup chopped cilantro (for garnish)

Instructions:

1. **Preheat Oven**: Preheat the oven to 350°F (175°C).
2. **Combine Ingredients**: In a large bowl, mix corn, mayonnaise, sour cream, cotija cheese, lime juice, chili powder, garlic powder, salt, and pepper.
3. **Transfer to Dish**: Pour into a greased 9x13-inch baking dish.
4. **Bake**: Bake for 25-30 minutes until bubbly and golden.
5. **Garnish**: Sprinkle with chopped cilantro before serving.

Seafood Pasta Bake

Ingredients:

- 8 oz pasta (penne or fusilli)
- 1 lb mixed seafood (shrimp, scallops, or crab)
- 1 jar (16 oz) Alfredo sauce
- 1 cup shredded mozzarella cheese
- 1/2 cup grated Parmesan cheese
- 1 teaspoon garlic powder
- Salt and pepper (to taste)

Instructions:

1. **Preheat Oven**: Preheat the oven to 375°F (190°C).
2. **Cook Pasta**: Boil pasta according to package instructions. Drain and set aside.
3. **Combine Ingredients**: In a large bowl, mix cooked pasta, seafood, Alfredo sauce, half of the mozzarella, garlic powder, salt, and pepper.
4. **Transfer to Dish**: Pour into a greased 9x13-inch baking dish.
5. **Top with Cheese**: Sprinkle remaining mozzarella and Parmesan on top.
6. **Bake**: Bake for 25-30 minutes until cheese is bubbly and golden.

Breakfast Casserole with Sausage

Ingredients:

- 1 lb breakfast sausage
- 8 eggs
- 2 cups milk
- 4 cups bread, cubed (preferably stale)
- 1 cup shredded cheese (cheddar or your choice)
- 1/2 cup chopped bell peppers
- Salt and pepper (to taste)

Instructions:

1. **Preheat Oven**: Preheat the oven to 350°F (175°C).
2. **Cook Sausage**: In a skillet, brown breakfast sausage until fully cooked. Drain excess fat.
3. **Whisk Eggs and Milk**: In a large bowl, whisk together eggs, milk, salt, and pepper.
4. **Combine Ingredients**: Add cubed bread, cooked sausage, bell peppers, and cheese to the egg mixture. Stir to combine.
5. **Transfer to Dish**: Pour into a greased 9x13-inch baking dish.
6. **Bake**: Bake for 30-35 minutes until set and golden.

Spinach and Feta Casserole

Ingredients:

- 4 cups fresh spinach (or 2 cups frozen)
- 1 cup crumbled feta cheese
- 1 cup ricotta cheese
- 4 eggs
- 1/2 cup milk
- 1 teaspoon garlic powder
- Salt and pepper (to taste)
- 1 cup breadcrumbs

Instructions:

1. **Preheat Oven**: Preheat the oven to 375°F (190°C).
2. **Prepare Spinach**: If using fresh spinach, sauté until wilted. Drain excess liquid.
3. **Combine Ingredients**: In a large bowl, mix spinach, feta, ricotta, eggs, milk, garlic powder, salt, and pepper.
4. **Transfer to Dish**: Pour into a greased 9x13-inch baking dish and sprinkle breadcrumbs on top.
5. **Bake**: Bake for 25-30 minutes until set and golden on top.

Baked Creamed Spinach Casserole

Ingredients:

- 4 cups fresh spinach (or 2 cups frozen)
- 1/2 cup cream cheese
- 1/2 cup sour cream
- 1/2 cup grated Parmesan cheese
- 1/2 cup shredded mozzarella cheese
- 1 teaspoon garlic powder
- Salt and pepper (to taste)

Instructions:

1. **Preheat Oven**: Preheat the oven to 350°F (175°C).
2. **Prepare Spinach**: Sauté fresh spinach until wilted. Drain excess liquid.
3. **Combine Ingredients**: In a large bowl, mix spinach, cream cheese, sour cream, Parmesan, garlic powder, salt, and pepper until well combined.
4. **Transfer to Dish**: Pour into a greased 9x13-inch baking dish and sprinkle mozzarella on top.
5. **Bake**: Bake for 20-25 minutes until heated through and bubbly.

These casseroles are flavorful and perfect for any occasion! Enjoy!

Italian Meatball Casserole

Ingredients:

- 1 lb Italian meatballs (frozen or homemade)
- 2 cups marinara sauce
- 8 oz pasta (penne or rotini)
- 1 cup shredded mozzarella cheese
- 1/2 cup grated Parmesan cheese
- 1 teaspoon Italian seasoning
- Fresh basil (for garnish)

Instructions:

1. **Preheat Oven**: Preheat the oven to 375°F (190°C).
2. **Cook Pasta**: Boil pasta according to package instructions. Drain and set aside.
3. **Combine Ingredients**: In a large bowl, mix cooked pasta, meatballs, marinara sauce, and Italian seasoning.
4. **Transfer to Dish**: Pour into a greased 9x13-inch baking dish. Sprinkle mozzarella and Parmesan on top.
5. **Bake**: Bake for 25-30 minutes until cheese is bubbly and golden.
6. **Garnish**: Sprinkle with fresh basil before serving.

Cranberry Chicken Casserole

Ingredients:

- 2 cups cooked chicken, shredded
- 1 can (14 oz) whole cranberry sauce
- 1 cup French fried onions
- 1 cup cooked rice
- 1/2 cup shredded cheddar cheese
- 1 teaspoon onion powder
- Salt and pepper (to taste)

Instructions:

1. **Preheat Oven**: Preheat the oven to 350°F (175°C).
2. **Combine Ingredients**: In a large bowl, mix shredded chicken, cranberry sauce, French fried onions, cooked rice, onion powder, salt, and pepper.
3. **Transfer to Dish**: Pour into a greased 9x13-inch baking dish and spread evenly.
4. **Top with Cheese**: Sprinkle cheddar cheese on top.
5. **Bake**: Bake for 25-30 minutes until heated through and golden.

Loaded Baked Potato Casserole

Ingredients:

- 4 cups baked potatoes, diced
- 1 cup sour cream
- 1/2 cup milk
- 1 cup shredded cheddar cheese
- 1/2 cup cooked bacon, crumbled
- 1/4 cup chopped green onions
- Salt and pepper (to taste)

Instructions:

1. **Preheat Oven**: Preheat the oven to 350°F (175°C).
2. **Combine Ingredients**: In a large bowl, mix diced potatoes, sour cream, milk, half of the cheese, bacon, green onions, salt, and pepper.
3. **Transfer to Dish**: Pour into a greased 9x13-inch baking dish and spread evenly.
4. **Top with Remaining Cheese**: Sprinkle remaining cheese on top.
5. **Bake**: Bake for 25-30 minutes until bubbly and golden.

Ratatouille Casserole

Ingredients:

- 1 eggplant, diced
- 2 zucchini, sliced
- 1 bell pepper, diced
- 1 onion, chopped
- 2 cups diced tomatoes (canned or fresh)
- 2 cloves garlic, minced
- 1 teaspoon dried basil
- 1 teaspoon dried oregano
- Salt and pepper (to taste)
- 1 cup shredded mozzarella cheese

Instructions:

1. **Preheat Oven**: Preheat the oven to 375°F (190°C).
2. **Sauté Vegetables**: In a skillet, sauté onion and garlic until softened. Add eggplant, zucchini, and bell pepper; cook until tender.
3. **Combine Ingredients**: In a large bowl, mix sautéed vegetables, tomatoes, basil, oregano, salt, and pepper.
4. **Transfer to Dish**: Pour into a greased 9x13-inch baking dish and sprinkle mozzarella on top.
5. **Bake**: Bake for 25-30 minutes until cheese is bubbly and golden.

BBQ Chicken Casserole

Ingredients:

- 2 cups cooked chicken, shredded
- 1 cup BBQ sauce
- 1 cup corn (canned or frozen)
- 1 cup shredded cheddar cheese
- 1/2 cup diced red onion
- 1 cup crushed tortilla chips

Instructions:

1. **Preheat Oven**: Preheat the oven to 350°F (175°C).
2. **Combine Ingredients**: In a large bowl, mix shredded chicken, BBQ sauce, corn, half of the cheese, red onion, and crushed tortilla chips.
3. **Transfer to Dish**: Pour into a greased 9x13-inch baking dish.
4. **Top with Remaining Cheese**: Sprinkle remaining cheese on top.
5. **Bake**: Bake for 25-30 minutes until heated through and cheese is melted.

Sloppy Joe Casserole

Ingredients:

- 1 lb ground beef
- 1 can (15 oz) sloppy joe sauce
- 1 cup cooked macaroni
- 1 cup shredded cheddar cheese
- 1/2 cup diced onion
- Salt and pepper (to taste)

Instructions:

1. **Preheat Oven**: Preheat the oven to 350°F (175°C).
2. **Brown Meat**: In a skillet, brown ground beef with onion. Drain excess fat.
3. **Combine Ingredients**: In a large bowl, mix cooked macaroni, cooked beef, sloppy joe sauce, salt, and pepper.
4. **Transfer to Dish**: Pour into a greased 9x13-inch baking dish and sprinkle cheese on top.
5. **Bake**: Bake for 25-30 minutes until heated through and cheese is bubbly.

Pizza Pasta Casserole

Ingredients:

- 8 oz pasta (penne or rotini)
- 1 lb Italian sausage, cooked and crumbled
- 1 jar (16 oz) pizza sauce
- 1 cup pepperoni slices
- 1 cup shredded mozzarella cheese
- 1/2 cup grated Parmesan cheese
- 1 teaspoon Italian seasoning

Instructions:

1. **Preheat Oven**: Preheat the oven to 375°F (190°C).
2. **Cook Pasta**: Boil pasta according to package instructions. Drain and set aside.
3. **Combine Ingredients**: In a large bowl, mix cooked pasta, sausage, pizza sauce, pepperoni, Italian seasoning, and half of the mozzarella.
4. **Transfer to Dish**: Pour into a greased 9x13-inch baking dish. Sprinkle remaining mozzarella and Parmesan on top.
5. **Bake**: Bake for 25-30 minutes until cheese is melted and bubbly.

Chicken Pot Pie Casserole

Ingredients:

- 2 cups cooked chicken, shredded
- 1 cup mixed vegetables (peas, carrots, corn)
- 1 can (10.5 oz) cream of chicken soup
- 1 cup chicken broth
- 1 teaspoon thyme
- 1 package (8 oz) refrigerated crescent rolls

Instructions:

1. **Preheat Oven**: Preheat the oven to 375°F (190°C).
2. **Combine Ingredients**: In a large bowl, mix shredded chicken, mixed vegetables, cream of chicken soup, chicken broth, and thyme.
3. **Transfer to Dish**: Pour into a greased 9x13-inch baking dish.
4. **Top with Crescent Rolls**: Unroll crescent rolls and lay them over the top of the mixture.
5. **Bake**: Bake for 25-30 minutes until the rolls are golden brown and the filling is bubbly.

These casseroles are perfect for cozy dinners and gatherings! Enjoy!

Cabbage Roll Casserole

Ingredients:

- 1 head cabbage, chopped
- 1 lb ground beef or turkey
- 1 cup uncooked rice
- 1 can (15 oz) tomato sauce
- 1 can (14.5 oz) diced tomatoes
- 1 onion, chopped
- 2 cloves garlic, minced
- 1 teaspoon paprika
- Salt and pepper (to taste)

Instructions:

1. **Preheat Oven**: Preheat the oven to 350°F (175°C).
2. **Brown Meat**: In a skillet, cook ground meat with onion and garlic until browned. Drain excess fat.
3. **Combine Ingredients**: In a large bowl, mix chopped cabbage, cooked meat, uncooked rice, tomato sauce, diced tomatoes, paprika, salt, and pepper.
4. **Transfer to Dish**: Pour into a greased 9x13-inch baking dish.
5. **Bake**: Cover with foil and bake for 60 minutes. Remove foil and bake for an additional 15 minutes.

Wild Rice and Mushroom Casserole

Ingredients:

- 1 cup wild rice, cooked
- 2 cups mushrooms, sliced
- 1 onion, chopped
- 1 cup vegetable broth
- 1 cup cream of mushroom soup
- 1 cup shredded cheddar cheese
- 1 teaspoon thyme
- Salt and pepper (to taste)

Instructions:

1. **Preheat Oven**: Preheat the oven to 350°F (175°C).
2. **Sauté Vegetables**: In a skillet, sauté mushrooms and onion until tender.
3. **Combine Ingredients**: In a large bowl, mix cooked wild rice, sautéed vegetables, vegetable broth, cream of mushroom soup, thyme, salt, and pepper.
4. **Transfer to Dish**: Pour into a greased 9x13-inch baking dish and sprinkle cheese on top.
5. **Bake**: Bake for 25-30 minutes until heated through and cheese is bubbly.

Shrimp and Grits Casserole

Ingredients:

- 1 cup grits, cooked
- 1 lb shrimp, peeled and deveined
- 1 cup shredded cheddar cheese
- 1/2 cup green onions, chopped
- 1/2 cup cooked bacon, crumbled
- 2 cups chicken broth
- 1 teaspoon Cajun seasoning
- Salt and pepper (to taste)

Instructions:

1. **Preheat Oven**: Preheat the oven to 350°F (175°C).
2. **Prepare Grits**: In a saucepan, combine grits and chicken broth. Cook until thickened. Stir in cheese, bacon, and green onions.
3. **Sauté Shrimp**: In a skillet, sauté shrimp with Cajun seasoning until cooked.
4. **Combine Ingredients**: In a large bowl, mix cooked grits and shrimp.
5. **Transfer to Dish**: Pour into a greased 9x13-inch baking dish.
6. **Bake**: Bake for 20-25 minutes until heated through.

Zucchini and Tomato Casserole

Ingredients:

- 3 medium zucchinis, sliced
- 4 tomatoes, sliced
- 1 onion, sliced
- 1 cup shredded mozzarella cheese
- 1/2 cup breadcrumbs
- 2 cloves garlic, minced
- 1 teaspoon dried basil
- Salt and pepper (to taste)

Instructions:

1. **Preheat Oven**: Preheat the oven to 375°F (190°C).
2. **Layer Vegetables**: In a greased 9x13-inch baking dish, layer zucchini, tomatoes, and onion. Sprinkle garlic, basil, salt, and pepper over layers.
3. **Top with Cheese**: Sprinkle breadcrumbs and mozzarella cheese on top.
4. **Bake**: Bake for 25-30 minutes until veggies are tender and cheese is bubbly.

French Onion Soup Casserole

Ingredients:

- 4 large onions, thinly sliced
- 4 cups beef broth
- 1/2 cup white wine (optional)
- 1 teaspoon thyme
- 1 cup crusty bread, cubed
- 1 cup shredded Gruyère cheese
- Salt and pepper (to taste)

Instructions:

1. **Preheat Oven**: Preheat the oven to 350°F (175°C).
2. **Sauté Onions**: In a large skillet, sauté onions until caramelized. Add wine (if using), broth, thyme, salt, and pepper.
3. **Combine Ingredients**: In a greased 9x13-inch baking dish, layer bread cubes, then pour onion mixture over the top.
4. **Top with Cheese**: Sprinkle Gruyère cheese on top.
5. **Bake**: Bake for 30-35 minutes until cheese is melted and golden.

Apple and Sausage Stuffing Casserole

Ingredients:

- 1 lb breakfast sausage
- 4 cups bread cubes (preferably stale)
- 2 cups apples, diced
- 1 cup celery, chopped
- 1 onion, chopped
- 1 teaspoon sage
- 1/2 cup chicken broth
- Salt and pepper (to taste)

Instructions:

1. **Preheat Oven**: Preheat the oven to 350°F (175°C).
2. **Cook Sausage**: In a skillet, brown the sausage, then drain excess fat.
3. **Combine Ingredients**: In a large bowl, mix bread cubes, cooked sausage, apples, celery, onion, sage, salt, pepper, and chicken broth.
4. **Transfer to Dish**: Pour into a greased 9x13-inch baking dish.
5. **Bake**: Bake for 25-30 minutes until heated through.

Lentil and Vegetable Casserole

Ingredients:

- 1 cup lentils, cooked
- 2 cups mixed vegetables (carrots, peas, corn)
- 1 can (15 oz) diced tomatoes
- 1 onion, chopped
- 1 teaspoon cumin
- 1/2 cup shredded cheese (optional)
- Salt and pepper (to taste)

Instructions:

1. **Preheat Oven**: Preheat the oven to 350°F (175°C).
2. **Combine Ingredients**: In a large bowl, mix cooked lentils, mixed vegetables, diced tomatoes, onion, cumin, salt, and pepper.
3. **Transfer to Dish**: Pour into a greased 9x13-inch baking dish. If using, sprinkle cheese on top.
4. **Bake**: Bake for 25-30 minutes until heated through.

Chocolate Chip Cookie Dough Casserole

Ingredients:

- 1 cup brown sugar
- 1/2 cup granulated sugar
- 1 cup butter, softened
- 2 cups flour
- 1 teaspoon vanilla extract
- 1 cup chocolate chips
- 2 eggs
- 1/2 teaspoon salt

Instructions:

1. **Preheat Oven**: Preheat the oven to 350°F (175°C).
2. **Mix Dough**: In a large bowl, cream together butter, brown sugar, and granulated sugar. Add eggs and vanilla; mix well. Gradually add flour and salt, then fold in chocolate chips.
3. **Transfer to Dish**: Pour dough into a greased 9x13-inch baking dish and spread evenly.
4. **Bake**: Bake for 25-30 minutes until golden brown. Let cool before serving.

These casseroles offer a variety of flavors and ingredients, perfect for any meal or occasion! Enjoy!

Cranberry and Orange Breakfast Casserole

Ingredients:

- 6 slices of bread, cubed
- 1 cup fresh cranberries (or dried)
- 1/2 cup orange juice
- 1/2 cup milk
- 4 eggs
- 1/2 teaspoon cinnamon
- 1/4 teaspoon nutmeg
- 1/2 cup maple syrup (optional)
- Zest of 1 orange

Instructions:

1. **Preheat Oven**: Preheat the oven to 350°F (175°C).
2. **Combine Ingredients**: In a large bowl, whisk together orange juice, milk, eggs, cinnamon, nutmeg, and orange zest. Add bread cubes and cranberries; mix well.
3. **Transfer to Dish**: Pour into a greased 9x13-inch baking dish. Drizzle maple syrup on top if desired.
4. **Bake**: Bake for 30-35 minutes until set and golden. Serve warm.

Butternut Squash and Kale Casserole

Ingredients:

- 4 cups butternut squash, cubed
- 2 cups kale, chopped
- 1 cup quinoa, cooked
- 1 onion, chopped
- 2 cloves garlic, minced
- 1 teaspoon thyme
- 1 cup shredded cheese (cheddar or Gruyère)
- Salt and pepper (to taste)

Instructions:

1. **Preheat Oven**: Preheat the oven to 375°F (190°C).
2. **Sauté Vegetables**: In a skillet, sauté onion and garlic until translucent. Add butternut squash and cook until tender. Stir in kale until wilted.
3. **Combine Ingredients**: In a large bowl, mix cooked quinoa, sautéed vegetables, thyme, salt, and pepper.
4. **Transfer to Dish**: Pour into a greased 9x13-inch baking dish. Sprinkle cheese on top.
5. **Bake**: Bake for 25-30 minutes until heated through and cheese is bubbly.

Greek Pastitsio Casserole

Ingredients:

- 1 lb ground beef or lamb
- 1 onion, chopped
- 2 cups pasta (ziti or penne), cooked
- 1 can (15 oz) crushed tomatoes
- 1 teaspoon cinnamon
- 1/2 teaspoon nutmeg
- 1 cup béchamel sauce
- 1 cup shredded mozzarella cheese
- Salt and pepper (to taste)

Instructions:

1. **Preheat Oven**: Preheat the oven to 350°F (175°C).
2. **Brown Meat**: In a skillet, cook ground meat with onion until browned. Drain excess fat. Add crushed tomatoes, cinnamon, nutmeg, salt, and pepper; simmer for 10 minutes.
3. **Layer Ingredients**: In a greased 9x13-inch baking dish, layer half the pasta, the meat sauce, and then the remaining pasta. Top with béchamel sauce and mozzarella.
4. **Bake**: Bake for 30-35 minutes until golden and bubbly.

Coconut Curry Rice Casserole

Ingredients:

- 2 cups cooked rice
- 1 can (14 oz) coconut milk
- 2 cups mixed vegetables (peas, carrots, bell peppers)
- 2 tablespoons curry powder
- 1 teaspoon ginger, minced
- 1 cup shredded coconut
- Salt and pepper (to taste)

Instructions:

1. **Preheat Oven**: Preheat the oven to 350°F (175°C).
2. **Combine Ingredients**: In a large bowl, mix cooked rice, coconut milk, mixed vegetables, curry powder, ginger, salt, and pepper.
3. **Transfer to Dish**: Pour into a greased 9x13-inch baking dish. Sprinkle shredded coconut on top.
4. **Bake**: Bake for 25-30 minutes until heated through.

Beef and Bean Enchilada Casserole

Ingredients:

- 1 lb ground beef
- 1 can (15 oz) black beans, drained and rinsed
- 1 can (10 oz) enchilada sauce
- 8 corn tortillas, cut into quarters
- 2 cups shredded cheese (cheddar or Mexican blend)
- 1 teaspoon cumin
- 1 teaspoon chili powder
- Salt and pepper (to taste)

Instructions:

1. **Preheat Oven**: Preheat the oven to 350°F (175°C).
2. **Brown Meat**: In a skillet, cook ground beef until browned. Drain excess fat. Stir in black beans, enchilada sauce, cumin, chili powder, salt, and pepper.
3. **Layer Ingredients**: In a greased 9x13-inch baking dish, layer half the tortilla quarters, half the beef mixture, and half the cheese. Repeat layers.
4. **Bake**: Bake for 25-30 minutes until heated through and cheese is bubbly.

Caprese Pasta Casserole

Ingredients:

- 8 oz pasta (penne or rotini), cooked
- 2 cups cherry tomatoes, halved
- 1 cup fresh mozzarella, cubed
- 1/2 cup fresh basil, chopped
- 1/4 cup balsamic glaze
- Salt and pepper (to taste)

Instructions:

1. **Preheat Oven**: Preheat the oven to 375°F (190°C).
2. **Combine Ingredients**: In a large bowl, mix cooked pasta, cherry tomatoes, mozzarella, basil, balsamic glaze, salt, and pepper.
3. **Transfer to Dish**: Pour into a greased 9x13-inch baking dish.
4. **Bake**: Bake for 20-25 minutes until heated through and cheese is melted.

Poppy Seed Chicken Casserole

Ingredients:

- 2 cups cooked chicken, shredded
- 1 can (10.5 oz) cream of chicken soup
- 1 cup sour cream
- 1 cup crushed crackers (such as Ritz)
- 1/4 cup poppy seeds
- 1/2 cup butter, melted

Instructions:

1. **Preheat Oven**: Preheat the oven to 350°F (175°C).
2. **Combine Ingredients**: In a large bowl, mix shredded chicken, cream of chicken soup, sour cream, and poppy seeds.
3. **Transfer to Dish**: Pour into a greased 9x13-inch baking dish. In a separate bowl, mix crushed crackers with melted butter and sprinkle on top.
4. **Bake**: Bake for 25-30 minutes until bubbly and golden.

Thai Peanut Chicken Casserole

Ingredients:

- 2 cups cooked chicken, shredded
- 1 cup cooked rice
- 1 cup broccoli florets
- 1/2 cup red bell pepper, sliced
- 1 cup peanut sauce
- 1/2 cup shredded carrots
- 1/4 cup chopped peanuts (for topping)
- Green onions (for garnish)

Instructions:

1. **Preheat Oven**: Preheat the oven to 350°F (175°C).
2. **Combine Ingredients**: In a large bowl, mix shredded chicken, cooked rice, broccoli, red bell pepper, peanut sauce, and shredded carrots.
3. **Transfer to Dish**: Pour into a greased 9x13-inch baking dish. Top with chopped peanuts.
4. **Bake**: Bake for 25-30 minutes until heated through. Garnish with green onions before serving.

These casseroles bring a delightful mix of flavors and are perfect for any meal! Enjoy!

Pumpkin and Sage Casserole

Ingredients:

- 2 cups pumpkin puree (fresh or canned)
- 1 cup ricotta cheese
- 1 cup cooked quinoa or rice
- 1/2 cup grated Parmesan cheese
- 2 eggs
- 2 teaspoons fresh sage, chopped (or 1 teaspoon dried sage)
- 1 teaspoon garlic powder
- Salt and pepper (to taste)
- 1/2 cup breadcrumbs (optional)

Instructions:

1. **Preheat Oven**: Preheat the oven to 350°F (175°C).
2. **Mix Ingredients**: In a large bowl, combine pumpkin puree, ricotta cheese, cooked quinoa, Parmesan cheese, eggs, sage, garlic powder, salt, and pepper. Mix well until smooth.
3. **Transfer to Dish**: Pour the mixture into a greased 9x13-inch baking dish. If desired, sprinkle breadcrumbs on top for added texture.
4. **Bake**: Bake for 30-35 minutes until the casserole is set and slightly golden on top.

Teriyaki Chicken Casserole

Ingredients:

- 2 cups cooked chicken, shredded
- 1 cup cooked rice (white or brown)
- 1 cup broccoli florets
- 1 cup carrots, sliced
- 1 cup teriyaki sauce
- 1 cup shredded mozzarella cheese
- 1/4 cup green onions, chopped (for garnish)
- Sesame seeds (for garnish)

Instructions:

1. **Preheat Oven**: Preheat the oven to 350°F (175°C).
2. **Combine Ingredients**: In a large bowl, mix shredded chicken, cooked rice, broccoli, carrots, and teriyaki sauce until well combined.
3. **Transfer to Dish**: Pour the mixture into a greased 9x13-inch baking dish. Sprinkle mozzarella cheese on top.
4. **Bake**: Bake for 25-30 minutes until the casserole is heated through and the cheese is bubbly and golden.
5. **Garnish**: Before serving, sprinkle with chopped green onions and sesame seeds.

Enjoy these flavorful casseroles!

www.ingramcontent.com/pod-product-compliance
Lightning Source LLC
LaVergne TN
LVHW081333060526
838201LV00055B/2608